# JOY H...

# PUT ON YOUR
# WAR COAT
## AND FIGHT!

*PUT ON YOUR WAR COAT*
by Joy Haney
© 2004


All Scripture quotations in this booklet are from the King
James Version of the Bible unless otherwise identified.

ISBN #1-880969-50-5

Printed in the United States of America

# CONTENTS

# FOREWORD
## Put on Your War Coat and Fight!

Isaiah 59:17 states: "For he put on righteousness as a breastplate, and an helmet of salvation upon his head; and he put on the garments of vengeance for clothing, and was clad with zeal as a cloke."

This sounds similar to some of the phrases used in Ephesians 6:13-17:

*Verse 13*: "Wherefore take unto you the whole armour of God, that ye may be able to withstand in the evil day, and have done all, to stand."

*Verse 14*: "Stand therefore, having your loins girt about with truth, and having on the breastplate of righteousness;"

*Verse 15*: "And your feet shod with the preparation of the gospel of peace;"

*Verse 16*: "Above all, taking the shield of faith, wherewith ye shall be able to quench all the fiery darts of the wicked."

*Verse 17*: "And take the helmet of salvation, and the sword of the Spirit, which is the word of God."

Garments of vengeance and a cloak of zeal: these are to be used in fighting against the wiles of the devil and evil powers.

It is time for the women to go to war in the spirit realm. Put on your war coat and fight. There was a literal fight in the Old Testament, and a woman was called to get involved in the winning of that war. The gist of the story is found in Judges 4:8-9: "And Barak said unto her, If thou wilt go with me, then I will go: but if thou wilt not go with me, then I will not go. And she said, I will surely go with thee: notwithstanding the journey that thou takest shall not be for thine honour; for the LORD shall sell Sisera into the hand of a woman. And Deborah arose, and went with Barak to Kedesh."

Deborah left her comfortable place under the palm tree and went to fight. She did this because the leader of the army refused to fight without her.

In these last days, God is calling the women to fight in the Spirit against principalities, evil spirits, hell, and sin. God needs us! The men need us! Our children need us! We ourselves need to fight. We must fight like never before.

In God's kingdom women are told to fight, to be strong. There are not two Bibles, one for the men and one for the women. There are not two different Holy Ghosts, one for men and one for women.

We fight daily against the devil, the desires of the flesh, sin and evil spirits that are sometimes manifested in people.

The fighting of the early church is noted in Hebrews 11:33-34: "Who through faith subdued kingdoms, wrought righteousness, obtained promises, stopped the mouths of lions, quenched the violence of fire, escaped the edge of the sword, out of weakness were made strong, waxed valiant in fight, turned to flight the armies of the aliens." They waxed valiant in fight! What a compliment from heaven. May the same be said of the modern-day church!

We do not fight with swords, knives, and guns, but it is a spiritual warfare that we are asked to fight. Heaven is on our side and we will win. The fight does get tough at times and hell seems to surround us on every side, but this is normal for a child of God.

When Jesus was asked of Pilate why He did not fight back with a sword when he was captured, John 18:36 records His response: "Jesus answered, My kingdom is not of this world: if my kingdom were of this world, then would my servants fight, that I should not be delivered to the Jews: but now is my kingdom not from hence."

The war has intensified, the enemy is nervous because he does not know how much longer he has. Hell has unleashed all its power and every demon is on the rampage, but as the end times wax worse and worse, the church must wax better and better in its diligent fight to overcome and win the victory!

# IT IS AN ABSOLUTE:

# YOU WILL FIGHT

# 1

# IT IS AN ABSOLUTE: YOU WILL FIGHT!

Face it, when you become a soldier in the Lord's army you will fight. II Timothy 3:12 states: "Yea, and all that will live godly in Christ Jesus shall suffer persecution." There will be hurtful things that happen, troubles will come, and hell will fight against the church.

It is an absolute. So instead of grumbling and complaining about it, as spiritual soldiers PUT ON YOUR WAR COAT and begin to fight as instructed in II Timothy 2:3-4:

*Verse 3*: "Thou therefore endure hardness, as a good soldier of Jesus Christ."

*Verse 4*: "No man [woman] that warreth entangleth himself [herself] with the affairs of this life; that he [she] may please him who hath chosen him [her] to be a soldier."

Paul instructed Timothy, as a man of God, to fight in I Timothy 6:12: "Fight the good fight of faith, lay hold on eternal life."

The ministers lead the way and we follow. They are the examples. If they must fight, we must fight.

We must realize the *HIM* that is with us and not be afraid to fight, as the children of Israel were under the leadership of Moses.

In Deuteronomy, Moses reiterated what happened

concerning the Israelites not taking the challenge to fight. Moses reminded them in Deuteronomy 1:29-32 what he had said earlier:

*Verse 29*: "Then I said unto you, Dread not, neither be afraid of them."

*Verse 30*: "The LORD your God which goeth before you, he shall fight for you, according to all that he did for you in Egypt before your eyes;"

*Verse 31*: "And in the wilderness, where thou hast seen how that the LORD thy God bare thee, as a man doth bear his son, in all the way that ye went, until ye came into this place."

*Verse 32*: "Yet in this thing ye did not believe the LORD your God."

We cannot afford to have the same thing said about us by our leader: Jesus Christ! He is asking us to fight and win, but He has promised to be with us always each step of the way.

Matthew 28:20: "Lo, I am with you alway, even unto the end of the world."

# WE MUST TAKE UP THE CROSS!

# 2

# WE MUST TAKE UP THE CROSS!

The fight is on: to pick up or not to pick up the cross. Ease beckons, laziness invites, and apathy seizes any soul who will take these lesser roads.

Jesus introduced the concept of cross-bearing in Matthew 16:24: "Then said Jesus unto his disciples, If any man [woman] will come after me, let him [her] deny himself [herself], and take up his [her] cross, and follow me."

Luke 9:24 pounds this truth home: "For whosoever will save his life shall lose it: but whosoever will lose his life for my sake, the same shall save it."

Picking up the cross is usually not convenient. The responsibility of the cross is contrary to our plans and the pampered life we would dream of leading.

The cross at work was reflected in the discourse of Matthew 25:35-36:

*Verse 35*: "For I was an hungred, and ye gave me meat: I was thirsty, and ye gave me drink: I was a stranger, and ye took me in:"

*Verse 36*: "Naked, and ye clothed me: I was sick, and ye visited me: I was in prison, and ye came unto me."

Jesus explained that when they were doing these things to the hurting people around them, they were really doing it unto Him, as stated in Matthew 25:40: "And the King shall answer and say unto them, Verily I say unto you, Inasmuch as ye have done it unto one of the least of these my brethren, ye have done it unto me."

Verse 41 states what will happen to those who do not do them: "Then shall he say also unto them on the left hand, Depart from me, ye cursed, into everlasting fire, prepared for the devil and his angels."

On the other hand, to those who did them He promised life eternal.

Accompanying these *cross assignments*, there is often pain, rejection, and fighting against the misunderstanding of people or associates. There is the pressure of finding enough money to fund the assignment, as well as the pressure of people who want to walk a lesser road trying to dissuade you from taking up your cross simply because it is a modern age with EASE written into the very fiber of everyday living.

Paul picked up his cross. He laid down his prestigious position among the elite religious group of his day, and when he did, all hell broke out for him. He was beaten, put in prison, shipwrecked and after naming all that he had been through, he inserted in II Corinthians 11:28 an even more vivid picture: "Beside those things that are without, that which cometh upon me daily, the care of all the churches."

He mentioned his troubles often. In I Corinthians 16:9 he stated: "For a great door and effectual is opened unto me, and there are many adversaries."

Then in II Corinthians 1:8 he shared this: "For we would not, brethren, have you ignorant of our trouble which come to us in Asia, that we were pressed out of measure, above strength, insomuch that we despaired even of life."

He did not end there. He summed it up when he came to the conclusion of his journey in II Timothy 4:7: "I have FOUGHT a good fight, I have finished my course, I have kept the faith." The summation of his whole life consisted of three things: "I have fought; I have finished; I have kept." He was saying, "Nothing defeated me. I won through Jesus Christ!"

# WE FIGHT
# AGAINST
# EVIL SPIRITS

# 3

# WE FIGHT AGAINST EVIL SPIRITS

Our fight is against principalities, powers, rulers of the darkness of the world and spiritual wickedness in high places as stated in Ephesians 6:10-13:

*Verse 10*: "Finally, my brethren, be strong in the Lord, and in the power of his might."

*Verse 11*: "Put on the whole armour of God, that ye may be able to stand against the wiles of the devil."

*Verse 12*: "For we wrestle not against flesh and blood, but against principalities, against powers, against the rulers of the darkness of this world, against spiritual wickedness in high places."

*Verse 13*: "Wherefore take unto you the whole armour of God, that ye may be able to withstand in the evil day, and having done all, to stand."

The evil one lurks in dark corners and does his best to cause the child of God to lose heart or to give up her stance, but no matter what happens, refuse to succumb to his tactics. Just stand strong on the Word, and you will win.

The devil is the prince of the air and is ever roving about in the earth trying to deceive and destroy as demonstrated in Job 1:7: "And the LORD said unto Satan, Whence comest thou? Then Satan answered the LORD, and said, From going to and fro in the earth, and from walking up and down in it."

I Corinthians 2:8 shares one of his evil concoctions: "Which none of the princes of this world knew:

for had they known it, they would not have crucified the Lord of glory."

These evil spirits are sometimes resident in men and women and are manifested in various ways in different places; but nevertheless, they are real.

The evil spirits were manifested in the brethren of Joseph. They were jealous of him and wanted to kill him. They could not stand his confidence and favor with his father, so they resorted to murder, but the older brother intervened and instead of killing him, they sold him to a band of Ishmeelites on their way to Egypt.

The good thing in all of this was the fact that "The Lord was with Joseph," as stated in Genesis 39:2, 21, & 23. The outcome of God being with Joseph was that he became the highest authority in the whole land of Egypt next to Pharaoh, and the summation is found in Genesis 50:20: "But as for you, ye thought evil against me; but God meant it unto good, to bring to pass, as it is this day, to save much people alive."

During these times we must ask for help and pray the following two prayers:

*Psalm 35:1*: "Plead my cause, O LORD, with them that strive with me: fight against them that fight against me."

*Psalm 40:14*: "Let them be ashamed and confounded together that seek after my soul to destroy it; let them be driven backward and put to shame that wish me evil."

We are in the flesh, but the battle is not hand-to-hand combat, it is Spirit against spirit as declared in II Corinthians 10:3: "For though we walk in the flesh, we do not war after the flesh."

There is power over the evil in the world through our Lord Jesus Christ as stated in Galatians 1:4: "Who gave himself for our sins, that he might deliver us from this present evil world, according to the will of God and our Father."

# WE FIGHT AGAINST CARNAL DESIRES

# 4

# WE FIGHT AGAINST CARNAL DESIRES

Paul states in I Corinthians 9:26-27 that keeping the body under subjection is a fight:

*Verse 26*: "I therefore so run, not as uncertainly; so FIGHT I, not as one that beateth the air:"

*Verse 27*: "But I keep under my body, and bring it into subjection."

It is war: the flesh against the Spirit. Romans 8:5 paints a picture of this war: "For they that are after the flesh do mind the things of the flesh; but they that are after the Spirit the things of the Spirit."

How does one win over the flesh? Romans 8:13 answers this: "For if ye live after the flesh, ye shall die: but if ye through the Spirit do mortify the deeds of the body, ye shall live."

It is "Not by might, nor by power, but by my spirit, saith the LORD of hosts" (Zechariah 4:6). "Likewise the Spirit also helpeth our infirmities: for we know not what we should pray for as we ought: but the Spirit itself maketh intercession for us with groanings which cannot be uttered" (Romans 8:26).

Through consistent prayer in the Spirit, the carnal desires of the flesh are brought under subjection. Each of us will determine what the outcome of the war will be. There are no losers with God. He will help those who are sincere and want to be victorious over carnal desires, for He knows who these people are as stated in II Timothy 2:19: "Nevertheless the foundation of

God standeth sure, having this seal, The Lord knoweth them that are his."

All of us will choose *who* will be our Master and we will choose *what* we will allow our Master to do with the material of our life whether we will be as gold, silver or wood as stated in II Timothy 2:20: "But in a great house there are not only vessels of gold and of silver, but also of wood and of earth; and some to honour, and some to dishonour."

It should be our desire to be a vessel described in verse 21: "a vessel unto honour, sanctified, and meet for the master's use, and prepared unto every good work."

Sanctification requires us working with God, allowing His Spirit to work in us. I Corinthians 6:11 demonstrates the power of God working in frail humanity through His Spirit: "And such were some of you: but ye are washed, but ye are sanctified, but ye are justified in the name of the Lord Jesus, and by the Spirit of our God."

There is a war going on! The following scriptures convey the war that goes on inside a person:

*James 4:1*: "From whence come wars and fightings among you? come they not hence, even of your lusts that **war** in your members?"

*I Peter 2:11*: "Dearly beloved, I beseech you as strangers and pilgrims, abstain from fleshly lusts, which **war** against the soul."

*Romans 7:23*: "But I see another law in my members, **warring** against the law of my mind, and bringing me into captivity to the law of sin which is in my members."

Colossians 3:5, 8-10, & 12 give explicit instructions of how to win in the war over self. First, we are to mortify or kill the flesh that is unlike Christ and to take off the dirty garments of anger, lying, etc., and put on the coat of righteousness.

*Verse 5*: "Mortify therefore your members which are upon the earth; fornication, uncleanness, inordinate affection, evil concupiscence, and covetousness, which is idolatry:"

*Verse 8*: "But now ye also put off all these; anger, wrath, malice, blasphemy, filthy communication out of your mouth."

*Verse 9*: "Lie not one to another, seeing that ye have put off the old man with his deeds;"

*Verse 10*: "And have put on the new man, which is renewed in knowledge after the image of him that created him:"

*Verse 12*: "Put on therefore, as the elect of God, holy and beloved, bowels of mercies, kindness, humbleness of mind, meekness, longsuffering."

Christ has made it possible to take off the coat that causes us to fail and to put on the coat of victory; therefore, we should greatly rejoice in this fact as portrayed in Isaiah 61:10: "I will greatly rejoice in the LORD, my soul shall be joyful in my God; for he hath clothed me with the garments of salvation, he hath covered me with the robe of righteousness."

# WE FIGHT
# AGAINST THE
# DEVIL

# 5

# WE FIGHT AGAINST THE DEVIL

Jesus said in John 10:10: "The thief cometh not, but for to steal, and to kill, and to destroy: I am come that they might have life, and that they might have it more abundantly."

Oh yes the thief may come, but we will do as Micah 7:7-8 says, "Therefore I will look unto the LORD; I will wait for the God of my salvation: my God will hear me. Rejoice not against me, O mine enemy: when I fall, I shall arise; when I sit in darkness, the LORD shall be a light unto me."

For Isaiah 54:17 declares: "No weapon that is formed against thee shall prosper."

Yes, we are in a fight as I Peter 5:8 states: "Be sober, be vigilant; because your adversary the devil, as a roaring lion, walketh about, seeking whom he may devour."

## THE DEVIL USES FEAR TACTICS

Lions roar to inflict fear in the heart of their victims. Likewise, the devil uses fear to seek to devour those who will let him, but it is a fact that fear is not of God for II Timothy 1:7 declares: "For God hath not given us the spirit of fear; but of power, and of love, and of a sound mind."

God knew Satan would try to overtake us through fear, so He has made provision in His Word to counteract fear as shown in the following scriptures:

*Isaiah 41:10*: "Fear thou not; for I am with thee: be not dismayed; for I am thy God: I will strengthen thee; yea, I will help thee; yea, I will uphold thee with the right hand of my righteousness."

*Psalm 27:1*: "The LORD is my light and my salvation; whom shall I fear? the LORD is the strength of my life; of whom shall I be afraid?"

*Joshua 1:9*: "Have not I commanded thee? Be strong and of a good courage; be not afraid, neither be thou dismayed: for the LORD thy God is with thee whithersoever thou goest."

We need to ever be aware that there are more with us than against us as Elisha told his fearful servant in II Kings 6:16: "And he answered, Fear not: for they that be with us are more than they that be with them."

In the Old Testament, Nehemiah stood to his feet when the people were surrounded by the enemy and thundered the words: "Be not ye afraid of them: remember the Lord, which is great and terrible, and fight for your brethren, your sons, and your daughters, your wives, and your houses."

"BE NOT AFRAID, BUT FIGHT" is still the battle cry today!

## THE DEVIL USES AN UNFORGIVING SPIRIT

Not only does Satan use fear to try to paralyze and intimidate God's children, but he also uses an unforgiving spirit as spoken of in II Corinthians 2:10-11:

*Verse 10*: "To whom ye forgive any thing, I forgive also: for if I forgave any thing, to whom I forgave it, for your sakes forgave I it in the person of Christ;"

*Verse 11*: "Lest Satan should get an advantage of us: for we are not ignorant of his devices."

We are told to resist his devices in James 4:7: "Submit yourselves therefore to God. Resist the devil, and he will flee from you."

James was writing not to sinners, but to the church. Several things he mentioned in the verses surrounding this scripture. He asked them, "Why are there wars and fighting among you?" He said, "You ask and receive not because you ask amiss." He stressed that envy is sin, and that we should humble ourselves because God resists the proud.

He continued in verses 11-12: "Speak not evil one of another, brethren. He that speaketh evil of his brother, and judgeth his brother, speaketh evil of the law, and judgeth the law: but if thou judge the law, thou art not a doer of the law, but a judge. There is one lawgiver, who is able to save and to destroy: who art thou that judgest another?"

When one Christian is angry with another Christian and there is division between them, this grieves the Holy Spirit of God. Once more Satan wins when this happens. We must fight against his evil ways and understand it is he that brings division and hatred.

We are instructed in Ephesians 4:29-32 to not let this happen and are shown very plainly how the Holy Spirit mourns over this:

*Verse 29*: "Let no corrupt communication proceed out of your mouth, but that which is good to the use of edifying, that it may minister grace unto the hearers."

*Verse 30*: "And grieve not the holy Spirit of God, whereby ye are sealed unto the day of redemption."

*Verse 31*: "Let all bitterness, and wrath, and anger, and clamour, and evil speaking, be put away from you, with all malice:"

*Verse 32*: "And be ye kind one to another, tenderhearted, forgiving one another, even as God for Christ's sake hath forgiven you."

Hateful spirits of envy and bitterness are called *devilish* in James 3:14-16:

*Verse 14*: "But if ye have bitter envying and strife in your hearts, glory not, and lie not against the truth."

*Verse 15*: "This wisdom descendeth not from above, but is earthly, sensual, devilish."

*Verse 16*: "For where envying and strife is, there is confusion and every evil work."

This is what the devil is all about: confusion, evil, hatred, sensuality, and bitterness. We must resist the devil. That means to oppose him, defy him, and refuse to accept what he suggests or imposes.

Jesus recognized the voice of Satan in the words that Peter spoke in Matthew 16, when Peter tried to keep the will of God from happening. He said, "Be it far from thee, Lord: this shall not be unto thee."

"But he turned, and said unto Peter, Get thee behind me, Satan: thou art an offence unto me: for thou savourest not the things that be of God, but those that be of men" (Matthew 16:23).

As Jesus rebuked Satan, so must we resist, defy, or oppose anything that is not in alignment with God's will and Word.

I John 4:4 needs to be paramount in our mind: "Ye are of God, little children, and have overcome them: because greater is he that is in you, than he that is in the world." GREATER IS HE THAT IS IN YOU!

# WAR A GOOD
# WARFARE

# 6

# WAR A GOOD WARFARE

In I Timothy 1:18 Paul admonished Timothy to WAR A GOOD WARFARE. What is the difference between a good and bad warfare? To war a good warfare, one must be prepared, be in good shape, have the proper weapons and follow the right leader.

God will help prepare us as we devour His Word, go in prayer to Him, and learn to listen to His voice. Our habits of spiritual disciplines will help keep us in good shape. We have powerful weapons and our leader is Jesus Christ.

Some may say, "I don't know how to war." That's OK. We have a good teacher.

Psalm 18:32-34 addresses this subject:

*Verse 32*: "It is God that girdeth me with strength, and maketh my way perfect."

*Verse 33*: "He maketh my feet like hinds' feet, and setteth me upon my high places."

*Verse 34*: "He teacheth my hands to war, so that a bow of steel is broken by mine arms."

Listen what happens when God teaches one how to fight:

*Verse 37*: "I have pursued mine enemies, and overtaken them; neither did I turn again till they were consumed."

*Verse 38*: "I have wounded them that they were not able to rise: they are fallen under my feet."

*Verse 39*: "For thou hast girded me with strength

unto the battle: thou hast subdued under me those that rose up against me."

He will teach His children how to fight and He should be praised for this as the psalmist stated in Psalm 144:1-2:

*Verse 1:* "Blessed be the LORD my strength, which teacheth my hands to war, and my fingers to fight:"

*Verse 2:* "My goodness, and my fortress; my high tower, and my deliverer; my shield, and he in whom I trust."

Even when we feel inadequate as Moses did, God will bear with us and teach us what to do as he told Moses in Exodus 4:15: "I will be with thy mouth, and with his mouth, and will teach you what ye shall do." Moses was called to be a deliverer of his people, and he had to fight against the power of Pharaoh and his stubbornness, but God prevailed as He always does.

When Moses did not know what to do, God always taught him and showed him the way. If we will trust Him, He will instruct us also as recorded in Proverbs 3:5-6:

*Verse 5:* "Trust in the LORD with all thine heart; and lean not unto thine own understanding."

*Verse 6:* "In all thy ways acknowledge him, and he shall direct thy paths."

Psalm 25:12: "What man is he that feareth the LORD? him shall he teach in the way that he shall choose."

The New Testament reveals that the Holy Ghost is a teacher as shown in the following verses:

*Luke 12:12:* "For the Holy Ghost shall teach you in the same hour what ye ought to say."

*John 14:26:* "But the Comforter, which is the Holy Ghost, whom the Father will send in my name, he shall teach you all things, and bring all things to your remembrance, whatsoever I have said unto you."

*I Corinthians 2:13:* "Which things also we speak,

not in the words which man's wisdom teacheth, but which the Holy Ghost teacheth; comparing spiritual things with spiritual."

When we stay full of the Holy Ghost, the Teacher is constantly teaching us how to war effectively against the evil that would seek to destroy.

# OUR POWERFUL
# WEAPONS

# 7

# OUR POWERFUL WEAPONS

II Corinthians 10:4 declares: "(For the weapons of our warfare are not carnal, but mighty through God to the pulling down of strong holds;)"

We fight with prayer and fasting, with praise, the Word, the Name, and God's Spirit! We are going to win as stated in I Corinthians 15:57-58: "But thanks be to God, which giveth us the victory through our Lord Jesus Christ. Therefore . . . be ye stedfast, unmoveable, always abounding in the work of the Lord, forasmuch as ye know that your labour is not in vain in the Lord."

Keep fighting, for you will be rewarded. Nothing can prevail against the church as stated in Matthew 16:18-19: "I will build my church; and the gates of hell shall not prevail against it. And I will give unto thee the keys of the kingdom of heaven: and whatsoever thou shalt bind on earth shall be bound in heaven: and whatsoever thou shalt loose on earth shall be loosed in heaven."

We have God on our side; we are going to win. Romans 8:31 declares: "What shall we then say to these things? If God be for us, who can be against us?"

He will give us power to fight against the devil, the flesh, sin and evil spirits!

He will fight for us! Isaiah 41:11-13 gives this promise:

*Verse 11*: "Behold, all they that were incensed

against thee shall be ashamed and confounded: they shall be as nothing; and they that strive with thee shall perish."

*Verse 12*: "Thou shalt seek them, and shalt not find them, even them that contended with thee: they that war against thee shall be as nothing, and as a thing of nought."

*Verse 13*: "For I the LORD thy God will hold thy right hand, saying unto thee, Fear not; I will help thee."

There is noise with wars; wars are not silent. When Joshua met Moses after he came down from the mount, he made the statement in Exodus 32:17: "There is a noise of war in the camp."

We need the noise of war to break out in the army of God's women like never before: the sound of prayer and praise.

The story in II Chronicles 20 demonstrates how Jehoshaphat fought with prayer and praise against the enemies that surrounded them. Acts 16:25 records how Paul and Silas fought back with prayer and praise when they were beaten and thrown in jail. We need to shake the very foundations of hell and fight back against the tactics of Satan with powerful prayer and praise.

The noise of travail needs to rise from the camp of the women in all our cities and churches across the land as stated in Isaiah 32:9, 11, 15:

*Verse 9*: "Rise up, ye women that are at ease; hear my voice, ye careless daughters; give ear unto my speech."

*Verse 11*: "Tremble, ye women that are at ease; be troubled, ye careless ones: strip you, and make you bare, and gird sackcloth upon your loins."

*Verse 15*: "Until the spirit be poured upon us from on high."

These scriptures, of course, are written to Israel, but the text is applicable to today's women. Women are not to literally strip themselves of clothing, but to strip themselves bare from the things that would hinder the Spirit from being poured out in our homes and churches. It is a call to humble ourselves before God in prayer, fasting, and travail, and to awaken to His call.

It is time as never before for the women to pick up the weapons and go into spiritual warfare and fight for our homes, our children, our churches, and the work of God around the world, for He has given us dynamite weapons with which to fight!

*The Word is powerful*: "For the word of God is quick, and powerful, and sharper than any twoedged sword, piercing even to the dividing asunder of soul and spirit, and of the joints and marrow, and is a discerner of the thoughts and intents of the heart" (Hebrews 4:12).

*Prayer is powerful*: "The effectual fervent prayer of a righteous man availeth much" (James 5:16).

*The Spirit is powerful*: "And my speech and my preaching was not with enticing words of man's wisdom, but in demonstration of the Spirit and of power" (I Corinthians 2:4).

*The Name is powerful*: "The name of the LORD is a strong tower: the righteous runneth into it, and is safe" (Proverbs 18:10). "That at the name of Jesus every knee should bow, of things in heaven, and things in earth, and things under the earth; and that every tongue should confess that Jesus Christ is Lord, to the glory of God the Father" (Philippians 2:10-11).

*The Blood is powerful*: "Forasmuch as ye know that ye were not redeemed with corruptible things, as silver and gold, from your vain conversation received by tradition from your fathers; but with the precious blood of Christ, as of a lamb without blemish and without spot: who verily was foreordained before the foundation of the world, but was manifest in these last times for you" (I Peter 1:18-20).

*His Power is powerful*: "And what is the exceeding

greatness of his power to us-ward who believe, according to the working of his mighty power" (Ephesians 1:19).

Revelation 12:11 gives further insight how the Christians will overcome Satan: "And they overcame him by the blood of the Lamb, and by the word of their testimony; and they loved not their lives unto the death."

Speak victory in the face of opposition and attacks from hell, and overcome with the word of your testimony and the powerful weapons of the Lord!

Speak it as Psalm 107:2 commands: "Let the redeemed of the LORD say so, whom he hath redeemed from the hand of the enemy."

# WE'LL CHANGE OUR WAR GARMENTS

# 8

# WE'LL CHANGE OUR
# WAR GARMENTS

Someday we are going to change our blood-spattered war garments for a gown of fine linen as declared in Revelation 19:7-8: "Let us be glad and rejoice, and give honour to him: for the marriage of the Lamb is come, and his wife hath made herself ready. And to her was granted that she should be arrayed in fine linen, clean and white."

There is a change coming as spoken of in I Corinthians 15:51-53:

*Verse 51*: "Behold, I shew you a mystery; We shall not all sleep, but we shall all be changed,"

*Verse 52*: "In a moment, in the twinkling of an eye, at the last trump: for the trumpet shall sound, and the dead shall be raised incorruptible, and we shall be changed."

*Verse 53*: "For this corruptible must put on incorruption, and this mortal must put on immortality."

Forevermore, we will be with the One who has a coat that is dipped in blood. Rev. 19:11-16 describes this phenomenon: "And I saw heaven opened, and behold a white horse; and he that sat upon him was called Faithful and True, and in righteousness he doth judge and make war. His eyes were as a flame of fire. . . . And he was clothed with a vesture dipped in blood: and his name is called The Word of God. And the armies which were in heaven followed him upon white horses, clothed in fine linen, white and clean. And out of his mouth goeth a sharp sword, that with it he should smite the nations: and he shall rule them with a rod of iron. . . . And he hath on his vesture and on his thigh a name written, KING OF KINGS AND LORD OF LORDS."

We are fighting for Him now, and He is fighting with us, but someday when we ride forth with the King of kings, he will do all the fighting and He will put the devil in his place.

We will not always need to fight against the flesh, sin, evil spirits and the devil, for there is coming an end to the fight. We are in the last rounds of the fight, and though we may be bloody and somewhat beat up, we are winning and the bell is going to sound and it will all be over very soon.

Keep fighting but keep your ear tuned for the signal: "For the Lord himself shall descend from heaven with a shout, with the voice of the archangel, and with the trump of God: and the dead in Christ shall rise first: then we which are alive and remain shall be caught up together with them in the clouds, to meet the Lord in the air: and so shall we ever be with the Lord" (I Thessalonians 4:16-17).

As our feet leave the ground, the change will come, and forever the devil will be under our feet. We will shout with the King of kings a shout of triumph as we lay our burdens down, lay our sword down, discard our coat of war, and float into the heavenlies to forever be with the Lord.

Philippians 3:20-21 will finally be fulfilled in us: "For our conversation is in heaven; from whence also we look for the Saviour, the Lord Jesus Christ: who shall change our vile body, that it may be fashioned like unto his glorious body, according to the working whereby he is able even to subdue all things unto himself."

# THE
# ENEMY
## WILL BE
# DESTROYED

# 9

# THE ENEMY WILL BE DESTROYED

Satan is the real "prince" of this world and organizer of "Babylon." Lucifer is his name, and he was the angel whom God exalted in heaven to be the leader over the music and worship. His fall is recorded in Isaiah 14:12-17:

*Verse 12*: "How art thou fallen from heaven, O Lucifer, son of the morning! how art thou cut down to the ground, which didst weaken the nations!"

*Verse 13*: "For thou hast said in thine heart, I will ascend into heaven, I will exalt my throne above the stars of God: I will sit also upon the mount of the congregation, in the sides of the north:"

*Verse 14*: "I will ascend above the heights of the clouds; I will be like the most High."

*Verse 15*: "Yet thou shalt be brought down to hell, to the sides of the pit."

*Verse 16*: "They that see thee shall narrowly look upon thee, and consider thee, saying, Is this the man that made the earth to tremble, that did shake kingdoms;"

*Verse 17*: "That made the world as a wilderness, and destroyed the cities thereof; that opened not the house of his prisoners?"

Satan has several descriptions:

He is known as the "accuser of the brethren" (Revelation 12:10).

He has been described as a "dragon" (Revelation

12:7).

He answers to "that old serpent, called the Devil" (Revelation 12:9).

What a diabolical nuisance he has been. What a pain. The trouble he has caused is endless. He is without a heart, devious, and full of evil. He is a liar and the father of lies. He deserves where he is going.

Revelation 20:10 describes his eternal place of abode: "And the devil that deceived them was cast into the lake of fire and brimstone, where the beast and the false prophet are, and shall be tormented day and night for ever and ever."

He that has brought you torment over your children who are unsaved, torment from carnal Christians, torment from the pressure of life, he is going to be tormented forever and ever with no relief.

# OUR REWARD
# FOR FIGHTING

# 10

# OUR REWARD FOR FIGHTING

Galatians 6:9 states: "And let us not be weary in well doing: for in due season we shall reap, if we faint not." There is a reaping day for services rendered and to those who overcome.

Hebrews 10:32 reminds the weary Christian to keep fighting: "But call to remembrance the former days, in which, after ye were illuminated, ye endured a great fight of afflictions."

The writer went on to encourage them to be confident in their reward:

*Verse 35*: "Cast not away therefore your confidence, which hath great recompence of reward."

*Verse 37*: "For yet a little while, and he that shall come will come, and will not tarry."

Paul wrote of our reward in II Timothy 4:8: "Henceforth there is laid up for me a crown of righteousness, which the Lord, the righteous judge, shall give me at that day: and not to me only, but unto all them also that love his appearing."

It is a delightful thought that while the devil is being tormented, we are going to be with Jesus in paradise and He will be giving us the perfect peace and joy that only He can give as described in Revelation 21:3-4:

*Verse 3*: "And I heard a great voice out of heaven saying, Behold, the tabernacle of God is with men, and he will dwell with them, and they shall be his people, and God himself shall be with them, and be their God."

*Verse 4*: "And God shall wipe away all tears from their eyes: and there shall be no more death, neither sorrow, nor crying, neither shall there be any more pain: for the former things are passed away."

The former things are gone forever: that means all the trials, tribulations, sins, sicknesses, strife, and Satan are all totally eradicated! No wonder the people in heaven will be crying Hallelujah!

Revelation 19:6 describes it: "And I heard as it were the voice of a great multitude, and as the voice of many waters, and as the voice of mighty thunderings, saying, Alleluia: for the Lord God omnipotent reigneth."

He is coming soon, as stated in Revelation 22:12: "And, behold, I come quickly; and my reward is with me, to give every man according as his work shall be."

The rewards are in His hands to give to those who overcome. In the seven churches, there was always a reward for those who overcame. These rewards are listed below:

*Revelation 2:7*: "To him that overcometh will I give to eat of the tree of life, which is in the midst of the paradise of God."

*Revelation 2:11*: "He that overcometh shall not be hurt of the second death."

*Revelation 2:17*: "To him that overcometh will I give to eat of the hidden manna, and will give him a white stone, and in the stone a new name written, which no man knoweth saving he that receiveth it."

*Revelation 2:26*: "And he that overcometh, and keepeth my works unto the end, to him will I give power over the nations."

*Revelation 3:5*: "He that overcometh, the same shall be clothed in white raiment; and I will not blot out his name out of the book of life, but I will confess his name before my Father, and before his angels."

*Revelation 3:12*: "Him that overcometh . . . I will write upon him my new name."

*Revelation 3:21*: "To him that overcometh will I grant to sit with me in my throne, even as I also overcame."

Revelation 22:14 pronounces a blessing upon those who fight a good fight and do as He commanded: "Blessed are they that do his commandments, that they may have right to the tree of life, and may enter in through the gates into the city."

What a city! It is described as having twelve gates of pearl and twelve foundations. The building of it consisted of jasper, pure gold, and precious stones of sapphire, chalcedony, emerald, sardonyx, sardius, chrysolite, beryl, topaz, chrysoprasus, jacinth and amethyst. The city needed no light bulbs for the light was supplied by the glory of God.

Wherever you are, whatever you are doing, no matter who you are, keep fighting the good fight of faith, and someday you will walk on streets of gold and live in exquisite, unmarred happiness. It will all be worth it when we see Jesus!

# I AM A SOLDIER

I am a soldier in the Army of my God.
The Lord Jesus Christ is my Commanding Officer.
The Holy Bible is my code of conduct.

Faith, Prayer and the Word
are my weapons of Warfare.
I have been taught by the Holy Spirit,
trained by experience,
tried by adversity,
and tested by fire.

I am a volunteer in this Army,
and I am enlisted for eternity.
I will either retire in this Army at the rapture
or die in this Army;
but I will not get out, sell out, be talked out.
I am faithful, capable, and dependable.

If my God needs me,
I am there.
If He needs me in Sunday school to teach children,
work with the youth, help adults, or just sit and
learn,
He can use me,
because I am there!

I am a soldier.
I am not a baby.
I do not need to be pampered,
petted, primed up, pumped up,
picked up, or pepped up.

I am a soldier. No one has to call me,
remind me,
write me, visit me,
entice me, or lure me.

I am a soldier.
I am not a wimp.
I am in place, saluting my King,
obeying His orders, praising His name,
and building His kingdom!

I am a soldier.
No one has to send me flowers,
gifts, food,
cards, candy,
or give me handouts.

I do not need to be cuddled, cradled,
cared for, or catered to.
I am committed!

I cannot have my feelings hurt bad enough to turn
me around.
I cannot be discouraged enough to turn me aside.
I cannot lose enough to cause me to quit.

When Jesus called me into this Army,
I had nothing.
If I end up with nothing,
I will still come out even.

I will win.
My God will supply all my needs.
I am more than a conqueror.
I will always triumph.
I can do all things through Christ.

I am a soldier.
Devils cannot defeat me.
People cannot disillusion me.
Weather cannot weary me.
Sickness cannot stop me.
Battles cannot beat me.
Money cannot buy me.

Governments cannot silence me,
and Hell cannot handle me!

I am a soldier.
Even death cannot destroy me.
For when my commander calls me from this battle-
field,
He will promote me to a captain
and then bring me back to rule this world with Him.

I am a soldier in the Army,
and I'm marching, claiming victory.
I will not give up.
I will not turn around.

I am a soldier,
marching Heaven bound.
Here I stand!

Will you stand with me?

Taken from: Email from "Inspirational
Pages at Cathy's World"